PONDERING
OF A
SOUL

PONDERING OF A SOUL

PATRICIA WALDEN

XULON PRESS

Xulon Press
2301 Lucien Way #415
Maitland, FL 32751
407.339.4217
www.xulonpress.com

ISBN-13: 978-1-6628-1754-0

DEDICATION

This book is dedicated to Richard Walden, my beloved
husband of 42 years. He was the most honest man
I have ever known and the wind beneath my wings.

Contents

GLORY

Glory, Glory, glory of things untold
As I close my eyes and behold a glimpse of
    Your glory unfold.

What joy—what peace
as within me You increase
I fall to my knees and bow, wondering how—how
You can love me here and now

You take me under Your wing
secure—Your praises I sing.
Your love knows no bounds, as my soul it surrounds.

MIRROR

When I look in the mirror, what do I see looking
    back at me.
The soul. as I'm known to man,
Or the spirit that I am.

The spirit that is in me
Be it dead or alive?
What do I believe?
How do I survive?

What will I put on-the-line
That will define my life in time.

I see a hurting person confused and lost...
I see a person willing to pay whatever the cost.

"YOU want me to what?
Repent and submit in love
For me does not calculate,
yet I cannot accept this fate.

Oh LORD help me to perceive and receive
The gift of your sacrifice
To believe and trust in YOU
For YOU only have paid the price.
Only YOU can see me through.

GOD WAITS ON ME

GOD waits on me. GOD waits on me!
How could this be—that GOD waits on me??

HIS desire is that none will be lost,
as in this world's troughs I'm tossed.
Yet, in mercy and grace
HE waits for me
to open my heart and eyes
and take my place

Many will scoff and deride.
Don't be among those who won't abide.
Don't live your life in apprehension,
though it is beyond comprehension

HIS great love—to send His Son from above
to take my sin and the wrath I deserve,
To give me this opportunity to serve,
To accept Him as my King and
the blessings this will bring,

The first is a grateful, understanding of
HIS mercy and grace from above and,
HIS everlasting, boundless love.

GOODIE TWO SHOES

Goodie-two-shoes is what they shout
As I turn to walk out.

Their jeers mean nothing to me
For my soul is my responsibility.

Please don't let my pride my candle hide.

DON'T WAIT—DON'T WAIT

It will be too late,
when you are outside the gate.

As I go thru today,
don't let my works be stubble and hay.
Only what's done in His name
shall survive the flame.

Let me always show
my hope and heaven's glow.
I am to forget about me,
if I am to live in Thee.
The news is great.
YOU are the WAY to heaven's gate.

YOU are the first fruits of reconciliation.
Belief in YOU is my soul's elation.

YOU who came and bled
took my sins upon Your head.
YOU paid the price for me so
I can be with YOU for eternity.

TRUCKING

I hear the eighteen- wheeler climb the steep and
    dusty hill.
See his bright lights gleaming in the dark
    night so still.

We too climb a steep and dusty hill.
Let HIS light shine before us in the dark night so still,
a beacon to all who will.

Come be a citizen of the heavenly chorus. Examine—
    examine and if it's remorse, listen to HIS voice.

GOD knows—GOD knows and HE gives you this choice.
Yea or nay what shall it be for your soul and eternity.

LOST SHEEP

When I look inside, I see me and not HIM
My heart grows dull and vision dim.
My pride puts HIM aside.

HE is important—yes,
But I live here and now and the world too
　　much adore.
It is not convenient to put HIM before.
Oh— woe –am I ashamed to mention HIS name?

If I don't claim HIM,
why would HE claim me?
HE does not play our games you see.

Thank you LORD—you understand, and
In great love still offer your wounded, pierced hand.

You are strong and I am stumbling and weak.
Yet, my soul You still seek
for I have become a lost sheep.
Gather me again unto your fold and
Let by my lips—Your glory be told.

BIBLE STUDY

Oh LORD as I take Your WORD in hand,
Let me read to understand.
Let me better know who you are—not just from afar.
Come deeper into my heart so,
I can better serve you than my start.

Help me seek the mystery,
Your wonderous Spirit.
To more fully perceive.

As basking in Your enduring love,
While looking above,
glimpse Your glorious throne
in our eternal home.

WHY

Clear your heart and mind
Of the clutter of this life
For peace and joy can be found
even in the midst of this strife.

Don't seek possessions for this is vain
Temporary at best.
Seek instead to join the blest.
Choose to believe the greatest
Gift you can conceive.

Quit asking GOD why.
Ask yourself instead.
Why you allow this other stuff into your head.
It is Satan's battle plan
To keep you in his hand but,

JESUS has pried Satan's hand open and
The chains of sin can be broken,
Believe and accept His work at the cross.
HE suffered and paid for the lost.

HE now holds the keys to death and hell.
Victory is ours—may peace within you dwell.

WAKE UP —
SMELL THE COFFEE

Rise up and get with it
There is much to be done.
We still have this race to be run.

You cannot in gulps—faith drink.
Standing beside the kitchen sink.

Read HIS words every morn
To gather strength for the burdens borne.

Let HIM live within you and pray.
HE will guide your actions this day.

VICTORY

Victory, victory Oh how sweet
To place the devil in retreat.

When we believe and trust in HIM,
HE who conquered death and sin

He will guide our steps.
He is the good shepherd
That cares and protects.
When we place our faith in Him,
This trust He will keep
For He does not abandon His sheep.

HE is alive – alive and waiting
The Day to gather us home
To joyously bow before His heavenly throne.

WARRIOR

HE provides the warrior in my soul
To stand against the evil foe.
Only my faith and trust in HIM,
keeps my light burning, however dim.

As I listen to HIS voice,
As HIS face I seek,
My flame burns brighter,
His strength fills me
as I grow weak.

One day this battle will end.
HE will come again
To take all HIS own,
To our heavenly home.

GO—GONE??

I feel so incompetent.
My get-up-and-go
got up and went.

Trying to do right
By my own might
Is a sure way to lose the fight.

My go is now with fuel injection.
HE is my fuel and protection.
All is not lost—
HE paid it all at the cross.
HE put it all on the line.
Let my belief in HIM make me HIS kind.

BRING IT ON

The gospel is implicit in all I do and say.
HE is the only way.
HE paid the price for me.
Broken and of trembling knee
before HIM I bow.

Let what comes— come for me now.
Nothing is lost, I have left my sins and heart
    at HIS cross

PAID

I don't have a Kleenex to wipe my tears.
GOD knows my fears.
HE gave it all at the cross.
Let me accept HIS suffering and loss.
HIS love, mercy and grace let me see.
HE who was blameless paid for me.

Let the Father's will be done.
Let my glory be HIS Son
No one else could pay the price
of HIS immortal sacrifice.
Let HIS spirit live in me.
Let my words proclaim
HIS gift and the glory of HIS name.

FREE

Free—free from shackles bound, and
The doubts and fears that forever hound.
The fear that I am not enough,
That I'll always fail when things get tough.

I am looking too much to me,
When only Your truth will set me free.
Your strength— not mine
can never come forth
until I step behind and,
clothed in your sacrifice and grace
take on whatever must be faced.

LOFTY MINDS

There are those of lofty minds
Who scoff and are unkind.
They put their faith in mortal man,
And will not believe the GREAT I AM.
Don't listen to the crowd,
For the broad way is walked by the proud.

Come, be set apart.
Let JESUS in your heart.
Come, walk the narrow way.
Listen to HIS voice—relent,
Turn your heart and repent.

Accept HIS magnificent sacrifice.
You will find HE will suffice.
You don't have to be perfect,
This is part of His gift to you, because HE is
    perfection.
Don't let His works be cast off by your deflection.
Open your heart. HIS words are true.
The only thing at stake is you,
And what's held for you above,
Thru the perfection of HIS love.
Come, be set apart.
Let HIM live in your heart.

SEEK HIM

It's about HIM—not about me.
HIS eternal Spirit to receive.
He who puts his hand to the plow
Shall not look back to the here and now.

Now can deceive and
take us from when we first believe.
Trust only what is true.
This is what HE is telling you.
How do you know truth from wrong?
The WORD will keep you strong.

Seek HIM always with your choice.
Learn to recognize HIS voice.
HE has said my sheep know my voice. Hear HIM.
Let us pray together—come take my hand and
    let us stand,
for all that is right in our FATHER'S sight.

BOTTOM LINE

As a business person
I believe in the bottom line
You can juggle things as you will and all appears fine
But faith you cannot just instill
Because truth does not abide the swill.

It is a difficult task
To yourself unmask.
In moments of deep reflection,
You see your need of deep introspection.
THINK—GOD gave you a mind.
Are you HIS kind?

You were created in HIS image for HIS love.
HE wants you to look to HIM
And not be guided by worldly whim.

Reach out, reach out accept HIS invitation
For HE loves His creation,
And came and died for us that is the bottom line.
Only faith and love WILL DEFINE
where you are at the end of time.

SWIM WITH THE SHARKS

I swam with the sharks but didn't fully succumb
His truth in me has helped me become
one who questions more the way of man,
and follow more the GREAT I AM
to look beyond today to see eternity
to really be all I can be.

When I believe and trust in HIM and HIS awesome gift,
my spirit and soul does lift.
It lifts my heart beyond this realm.
I know HE is at the helm.
HE will guide my path
For I was not created for wrath.
My future lies in glory above.
My soul is surrounded with grace and love.

HE IS THE WAY

Happy, happy day!!
HE is the WAY.
HE doesn't say get out of my way but
Follow me today, I am the way.
HE forgives any sin when we trust and believe in Him
HE died and arose so we could live.
HE has paid our sin HE will take us in.
What more can HE give?

How can we perceive the need to believe.
HIS gift of forgiveness and eternal life,
HE can carry us thru the strife
To know we have a place,
To one day see His face

Let the angels rejoice
Because you now hear His voice.
His promises are true—never fear it
Can you hear it?
Oh, happy, happy day
To one day sing
Praises to our KING

I KNOW

Let me serve your kingdom on this earth.
This is the reason for my birth.
Let all I touch and say
As I go through today
be that which glorifies You in every way.
Let your truth shine from me,
not only here and now
but through eternity.

I cannot do this on my own
For I am mortal and You are not
Give me the strength I have not got.
Carry me through to before your throne
your glory within me is shown.
I know You have a plan for my life.
Keep my eyes on You in all this strife,

You do not force it.
I have a choice.
You have said my sheep know my voice.
Because of Your sacrifice,
I know I have a life.
I know—I know because You have told me so.

UNDER HIS WING

I am confused,
in life's winds tossed,
twirling around
for all looks lost.

I cry out.
You take my hand and
bring me on firm ground to stand
Upon Your truth,
Your shed blood,
Your body broken
You overcame death and hell with Your sacrifice.
You paid a horrible price

Your HOLY love,
which could only come from above,
You brought down
to my brokenness surround,
You fold me under Your wing
So this worthless one can one day sing
Praises to my LORD and KING.

Let me accept what you have done.
Let not my song be unsung.

DON'T BE AN ALMOST

I believe in You but
I'm not abiding in You.
It's inconvenient and
more than I worldly want.
Though I'm alive,
my spirit grows gaunt.

It is worse for me than for those who deny
    and flaunt.
I haven't taken my prideful soul to it's knees.
My mind has accepted and my heart agrees but
my pride makes this a token.
This is why I am so broken.

Why don't I understand?
You take me just as I am.
If I fully place my trust and faith in You,
Without reservation, without hesitation
You will guide and see me through.

You take my brokenness and
will forgive so I may live.
Faith the size of a mustard seed
is all I need to
bend my knee and
grow to a great tree.

HIS YOKE IS LIGHT

HE has said, "My yoke is light".
Because HE carries the load.
HE wants to be paired with me as I travel this road.

HE will always be by my side as
HIS love and commandments in my heart abide.
My soul, my spirit leap and rejoice
as I listen for HIS voice.

HE has said the path can be rough.
Through Him I find strength and
courage to be tough and
stand my ground.
HE is the foundation my faith is found.
I have accepted the gift of HIS awesome sacrifice.
HIS blood has cleansed me of worldly vice,
And bestowed in me a new life.

HE is the GREAT I AM and meager I be
I seek to serve HIM on earth and into eternity.
HE has said I am HIS own.
HE will never leave me alone.

PRECIOUS HOPE

HIS precious blood HE has shed
To purchase you and me from the dead.
Dead in sin but HE has taken it within,
All the humiliation and shame
HE did not suffer in vain.
HE instead of me.

HE paid the price
To give life and
Peace everlasting.
Believe Him
Trust Him
Know Him

Oh, what you will hear Him say
When you read and meditate on His words each day.
Know you have found your solid ground,
your fortress, your healing, your protector,
    your peace.
May His blessings on you abound.

Put HIM first and
Never again thirst
for truth and right.
Walk in what's good in HIS sight and
All will unfold in heaven's glory told.

YADA, YADA, YADA

You can't communicate with people
when their eyes glaze over
and they are thinking yada, yada, yada.

Let me speak staccato.
HE came.
HE lived.
HE died—crucified.
HE arose.
HE lives.
HE lives.
HE comes again

Don't risk everything remaining in sin.
You have the choice.
Accept HIS blood as the price,
HE paid to break us free.
HE bought you and me for eternity.

Accept HIS gift or not.
If no, then all is naught.
Go about your way but
You will stand before HIM one day.

LONELY

Sometimes I feel so lonely without love.
I need to talk with someone.
Then I remember HE is someone—
    the one who is alive and above.
The only One to whom hurt and cares I can bring.
My Savior and my King.

When I accept HIS gift and grace,
My trust in HIM alone will place
In repentance, submission and love,
I feel HIS outpouring from above.
I feel my soul begin to lift.
Help me LORD to never again drift.

To always keep you in my sight and
Help me do what you have shown is right.
To not only love you but my fellow man
This is the will of The GREAT I AM.

HOMELESS

Alone, alone
it seems I have no home.
Hallelujah!!
YOU have prepared a home for me
on heavenly grounds.
Your love knows no bounds.
YOU paid the price for me at calvary
To live with YOU through eternity.

When I believed, repented
and was baptized in Your name.
YOU adopted me
as part of Your heavenly family.
Your glory I now proclaim.

Submission to YOU is
the wisest thing I have ever done.
Now this earthly course I can run
With no fear of death and hell.
I have a home in which to dwell.

NOT FANTASY

YOU and Your Kingdom are not fantasy
YOU are the <u>only true reality</u>.

Oh LORD strip me bare.
Help me take everything from my life that
should not be there.

Let me each day
Bow on humble knee to pray
in gratitude and awe.
Let me always harken to your call.

Let me kneel to Thee before your throne.
Precious LORD
Carry me home.

NEVER BEND

Sometimes it feels like your life is in tatters.
Put your trust in what really, really matters.

There are those who think they are smarter
But my faith is not up for barter.
My faith, my trust is in HIM.
Though things around may look grim,
My focus shall remain on HIM.

I follow HIS command
to love GOD and my fellow man.
When I live in HIS name and
help another do the same
We can walk on water as HIS son or daughter.

Though waves of strife surround,
I know where my strength is found.
Only through HIM shall I ascend.
On this truth I shall never bend.

MY SKY OF BLUE

Thank You Lord for the sun on my face and
    sky of blue.
Let Your will be in whatever I do.
Thank You Lord for this breath.
Thank You Lord for your death.

You created us in your image. You took the mortal
    form of your creation
which is beyond our feeble imagination.
fully God yet fully man – You the Alpha and Omega,
    the Great I AM

Such love is almost beyond belief.
You dwelt among us.
You came to redeem us from the thief.

Your earthly body bleeding and torn,
Our transgressions You have borne.
As Satan snarls and writhes around,
Your grace will the more abound.

Why don't we see
through You lies victory.
Only a return of this great love
with pride and self laid down
will earn faithfulness' crown.

So we may thank You face-to-face
for your loving mercy and grace.

MARRIAGE

God made us one from two.
So this world we could subdue and
hold onto life. through trouble, toil and strife
As helpmates, hand in hand
Working together to defeat the Devil's plan.

Our Lord has firmly placed our feet
to not accept the Devil's deceit.
My love respects and honors me,
And his spirit and love of God I see.

It's not perfect because it's a human relationship, but
we always hold our grip.
Together we can conquer all
As was meant before the fall.

Though individually we will be judged
For the path we have trudged.
As soulmates we stand our ground,
And God's blessings shall abound.

FEAR OF FAILURE

Fear of failure is a sure way to fail.
Fear makes you frail.
Fear places you in a jail
That you make.
Why ponder—I can't get a break.

Step out from the shroud of doubt.
Step out
Step out.

When you say I'm not good enough.
You are only repeating the Devil's stuff
There is no magic bean
Put your trust in glory now unseen.

Quit worrying about the thoughts of man.
Consider only the way of THE GREAT I AM.
As faith grows stronger, and
You come out of your comfort zone,
You can walk as one of His own.

ODD ONE OUT

I don't want to be the odd one out.
I need to conform
To be part of the norm.
They say this is what it is all about.
Man says be this or that.
They deny the SON HE begat.

GOD says He wants each and everyone
to come to Him thru His Son.

Come be set apart.
Accept Christ in your heart,
Not just mentally but
With heartfelt reality
Of this desire for more.
Come in repentance.
He waits at the door.

God wants us to be the odd one out
And because of His gift
To stand and His praises shout.
So others will know
This wonderous peace
He has given you,
Can be theirs too.

ONE NAME

HOPE can be summarized in one word
In one name—Jesus.
The Word, the Way, the Truth and the Life.
Only through one name is hope given and
In His name we should be living.

There are those who deny
His right to hear our cry.
He is exclusive as He is the only way.
He is wholly inclusive to all who hear and believe
What He has to say.

He gave all on the cross,
To purchase us from the lost.
Today is the day, please don't delay.
Don't wait. Don't risk being
Outside heaven's gate.

Why do you chaff at who I call friend
And will not abandon.
I know He will be here for me
to the very end and thru eternity.
Not a denomination,
Nor a congregation
Only in HIS remediation
lies my hope.

MUD PUDDLES

I'm thinking what is at stake.
You are thinking—give me a break.

Jumping in the same mud puddle never
    solved a thing.
Step out of the mud and see
What HIS grace will bring.

Oh LORD, I cannot get this mud off.
It just won't slough,
Take me from this trough.

I feel guilt and remorse
To have sinned against You, and
Ask forgiveness and for your righteousness
To within my heart imbue.

Accept me LORD,
Let me be buried in water and washed in your blood
To arise anew,
To serve only You.

UNTIL THE DAY

All I know is with my last breath
I will again thank Him for His death.
The price He paid for me to be with Him in eternity.

Though feeble and fumbling
I often fail.
I know His sacrifice will prevail.

When I come on bended knee,
Heart pierced for the sin I've done,
Or allowed myself to see
HE will forgive
That I might live.

My trust is in the glory of His name.
HE has already taken my blame.

CPSIA information can be obtained
at www.ICGtesting.com
Printed in the USA
LVHW072127040621
689408LV00002B/3